How to Make BALLOON Models

Models by Ted Lumby
Edited by Annette Love
Photography by Alan Roberts
Design by Gina Read

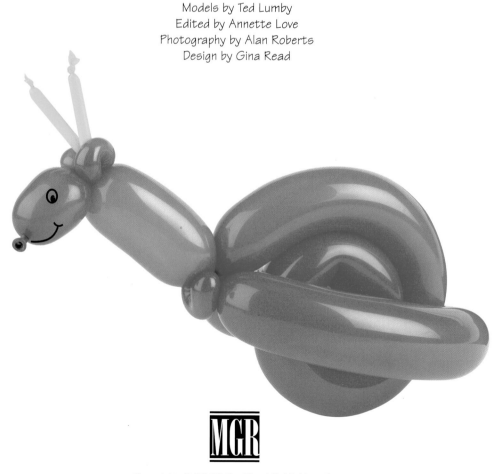

MGR

Contents

Tricks of the Trade   4

Jolly Giraffe   6

Mouse Magic   8

Black Swan   9

High Flyer   10

Fishing Trip   12

Pet Poodle   14

Sword and Shield   16

Flower Power   18

Delightful Daisy   19

Terrible Tiger   20

Penguin Parade   22

Prize Pony   24

Ladybird Trail	26
Speedy Snail	27
Party Time!	28
Scary Spider	30
Daring Dog	32
Space Bug	34
Batmania	36
Sea Horse	38
Rock Lobster	40
Dizzy Dragonfly	42
Baby Elephant	44
Jungle Fever	46
Exotic Octopus	48

Tricks of the Trade

Have you ever seen anyone make a balloon model? It's fantastic what you can make out of a balloon, and all in a matter of seconds. With a little practice, you'll be making aeroplanes, elephants, and lots more besides!

In your pack you will find a balloon pump and four sorts of balloons: long ones, long thin ones, large round ones and small round ones. When you blow up a balloon, tie a knot when it reaches the right size. To deflate a balloon, ask an adult to snip a hole in the end, leaving enough latex to tie a knot. Don't let go until the knot is secure! Follow the measurements provided in the steps, but please remember that they only act as a guide to making the models.

Always ask an adult to cut off any untidy bits of leftover balloon with a pair of scissors.
Store this pack away neatly when you have finished modelling, and keep it in a safe place where young children can't reach it.
Before you start making any of the models, take a long balloon from your pack and practise the twists shown here. Then, you'll be all set to make this collection of exciting and original models!

Lock Twist

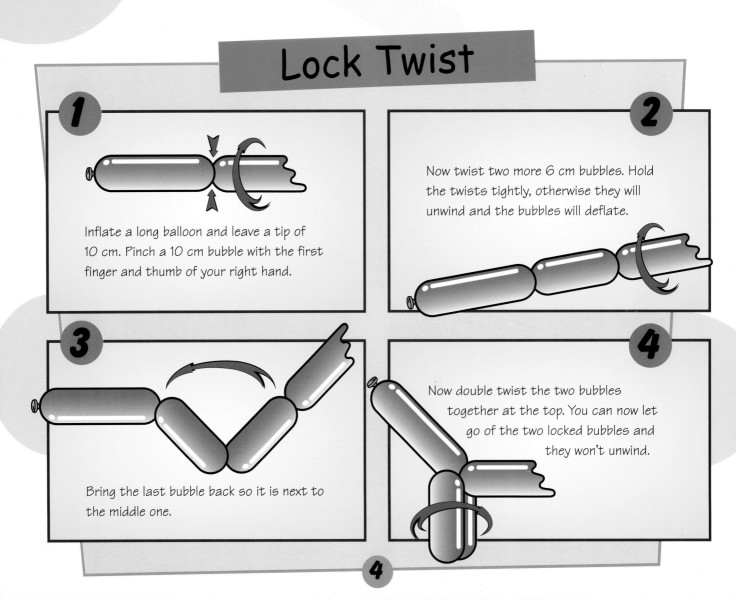

1 Inflate a long balloon and leave a tip of 10 cm. Pinch a 10 cm bubble with the first finger and thumb of your right hand.

2 Now twist two more 6 cm bubbles. Hold the twists tightly, otherwise they will unwind and the bubbles will deflate.

3 Bring the last bubble back so it is next to the middle one.

4 Now double twist the two bubbles together at the top. You can now let go of the two locked bubbles and they won't unwind.

Ear Twist

1
Twist a 12 cm bubble, followed by a 6 cm bubble. Hold the first twist between the two bubbles, then fold the second bubble back to the twist.

2
The twists at the beginning and end of the bubble should be next to each other. Now fix the bubble in a 'C' shape by twisting both ends of the bubble together.

Apple Twist

1
Inflate a 3 cm bubble in a long balloon and tie a knot. Hold the bubble in one hand. With the first finger of your other hand, press the knot back inside the bubble.

2
Push the knot all the way to the end of the bubble so that it touches the beginning of the deflated section, or 'stem'.

3
Grasp the knot through the wall of the bubble and remove your finger – the balloon may stick to you, so take care not to let go of the main bubble! To fix the knot in the stem balloon, double twist the new bubble.

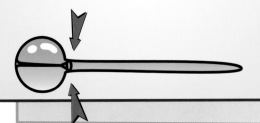

4
To make a good apple shape, hold the stem and push the knot back into the bubble, where the air pressure inside the balloon will hold it tightly in position.

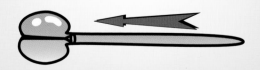

Jolly Giraffe

You'll be amazed at how easy it is to make this jolly giraffe – if you can't remember all the twists, just look back to the previous page.

YOU WILL NEED:

One long balloon

Felt pen

1

Blow up the balloon and leave a 10 cm tip at the end. Tie a knot. To form the head, twist a 5 cm bubble at the knotted end.

2

Now twist two 2 cm bubbles. These will become the giraffe's ears. Don't let go, or you'll have to start from the beginning again!

3

Ear twist the first 2 cm bubble at the top of the head. Make the second ear in the same way as the first.

4

Next, twist a 30 cm bubble for the neck, followed by two 12 cm bubbles to make the legs.

Tip
You can change the shape of the giraffe's head by gently pulling on the knot and squeezing the bubble at the same time.

5

Lock twist the last two bubbles together at the base of the neck to make the front legs.

6

Create the body with an 8 cm bubble, then form the rear legs by lock twisting two 10 cm bubbles together as before.

7

Push the remainder of the balloon up between the rear legs to form the tail. Use a felt pen to add eyes, a mouth and wild giraffe markings!

Tip
Gently squeeze and bend the neck bubble to give your giraffe a more natural look.

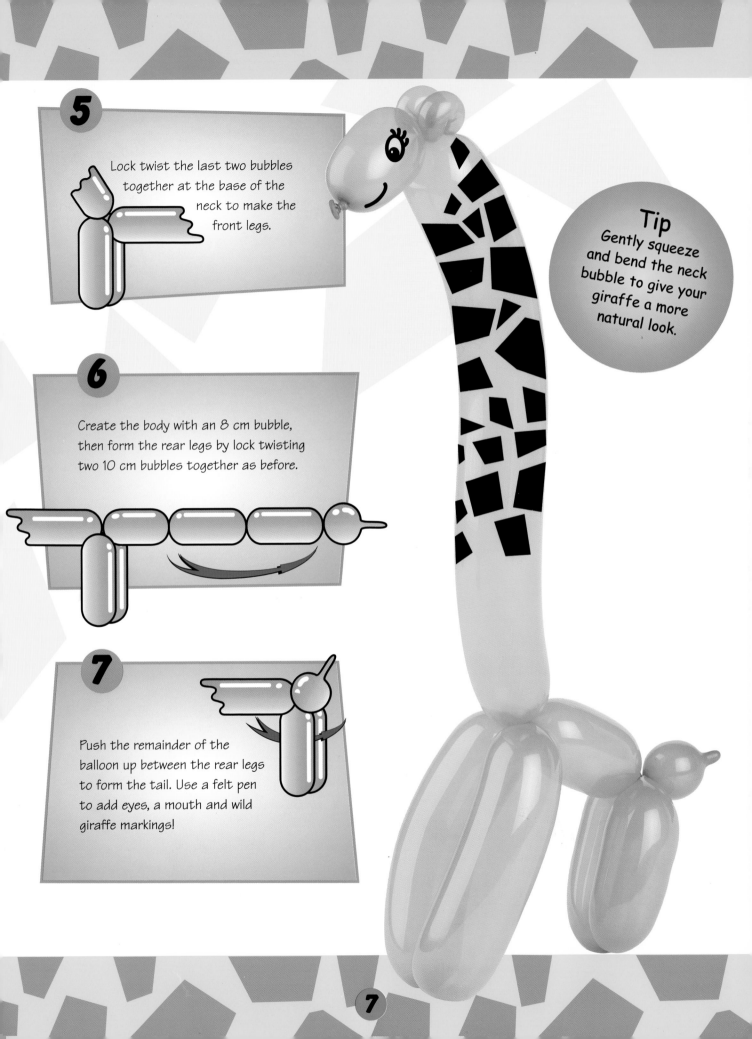

Mouse Magic

People won't believe their eyes when you magic this mouse (almost) out of thin air!

YOU WILL NEED:

One long balloon

Felt pen

1 Inflate the balloon to 18 cm. Twist three 3 cm bubbles ready to make the head and ears. Lock twist the last two bubbles together. Well done, the head is already finished!

2 Hold the head and twist another three 3 cm bubbles. Now lock twist the last two together for the mouse's front legs.

3 The rest of the body is made by twisting another three 3 cm bubbles. Make sure there is still a little bubble of air left after the last one.

4 Lock twist the last two 3 cm bubbles together to form the hind legs. Make the tail by pushing the last bubble up between the back legs. Bring your mouse to life by adding a cheeky face with a felt pen.

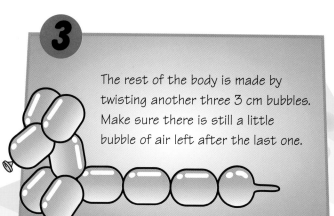
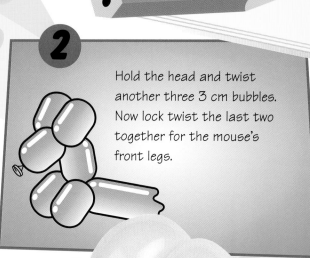
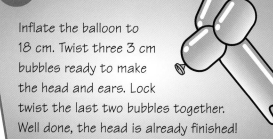

Black Swan

This graceful black swan is so quick to make – it only needs a single twist. Why not make a white swan too?

YOU WILL NEED:
One long balloon
White paper
Scissors
Felt pen
Glue

1

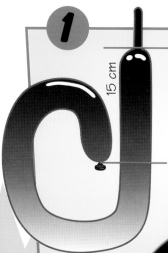

15 cm

Inflate your balloon to 60 cm and tie a knot. Hold the knotted end and bring the tip of the balloon round to make a loop, overlapping the knotted end by 15 cm.

2

Squeeze and lock twist the three inflated lengths of the balloon together. You will now have a long neck and two loops to make the main body.

Tip
Try not to inflate the tip all the way to the end, as it forms the swan's beak.

3

Tuck one loop up through the other to form the swan's wings and body. Push the base of the swan's neck into the lock twists at the front of the body to hold it upright.

4

Hold the deflated tip of the balloon at the front of the swan's neck and gently squeeze some air up into it. This will curve the neck nicely and also form the head. Glue on paper cut outs for the eyes and wings.

9

High Flyer

When you have mastered how to create this aeroplane, you will be able to make all different types, simply by changing the proportions.

YOU WILL NEED:

Two long balloons

Felt pen

Scissors

1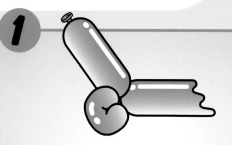

Inflate a blue balloon and leave a 15 cm tip. Begin the plane's tail by twisting a 7 cm bubble, followed by a 3 cm bubble, which is ear twisted.

2

Twist two 8 cm bubbles and ear twist each one. Position them either side of the tail. Next, twist a 22 cm bubble.

3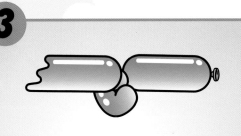

To complete the fuselage, ear twist a 3 cm bubble, then twist a 15 cm bubble. Make sure that the small bubble is on the underside. Deflate, tie off, tidy and save the scraps; refer back to page four for more help.

4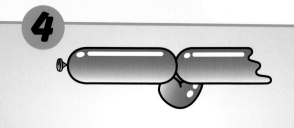

Now take a lilac balloon and inflate it to leave a 15 cm tip. Twist a 24 cm bubble, then ear twist a 3 cm bubble.

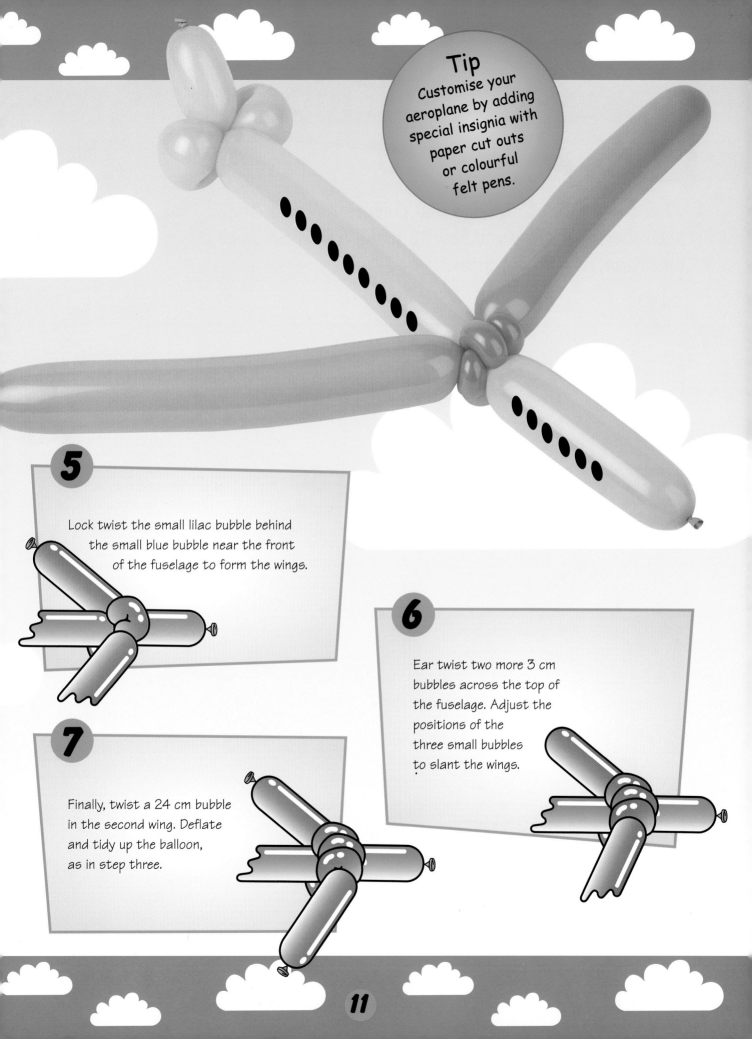

5

Lock twist the small lilac bubble behind the small blue bubble near the front of the fuselage to form the wings.

6

Ear twist two more 3 cm bubbles across the top of the fuselage. Adjust the positions of the three small bubbles to slant the wings.

7

Finally, twist a 24 cm bubble in the second wing. Deflate and tidy up the balloon, as in step three.

Fishing Trip

There are lots of strange and colourful fish in the sea – here we show you how to make a Red Snapper, and then, how to catch it!

1

Inflate the long balloon, leaving a 3 cm tip. Now gently squeeze the air to the end to fill the tip.

2

Make a twist halfway along the balloon. Twist a 4 cm bubble either side of the centre twist, then ear twist each bubble to make the lips.

3

Curve the two ends of the balloon towards each other. Lock twist them together 18 cm from the ends to make tail fins.

4

Finish the tail by twisting
a 4 cm bubble in one fin,
close to the body.
Ear twist it at the base.
Repeat with the other tail fin.

5

Inflate the round balloon so it is almost
full, then tie off. Tie the knot of the round
balloon to the ear twists of the fish's
tail. Fit the round
balloon into the
body space.

6

Inflate a long balloon to leave a 3 cm tip.
Twist a 12 cm bubble, then ear twist an
8 cm bubble. Now ear twist a 12 cm
bubble. Push the smaller ear twisted
bubble inside it to form the reel.

Tip
Make an underwater
paradise full of
tropical rainbow
fish – all you need are
lots of brightly
coloured balloons!

7

Ear twist a 3 cm bubble to sit on top of
the reel. This also locks the twists. Finally,
tie an uninflated balloon to the tip to act
as the line. Good luck with your fishing!

Pet Poodle

If you've ever wanted a pet dog, now is your chance to have one. The real bonus is that they don't need a lot of looking after!

YOU WILL NEED:

One long balloon

Felt pen

1

Inflate the balloon leaving only a 15 cm tip and tie a knot. Twist an 8 cm bubble, followed by three 4 cm bubbles.

2

To make the poodle's head, lock twist the first and last small bubbles to form a loop. Push the knotted end partway through the loop. Form the neck by twisting a 7 cm bubble.

3

Now twist an 8 cm bubble, followed by two 2 cm bubbles, then another 8 cm bubble. Hold them securely!

4

The next step is to lock twist the two longer bubbles together to make the poodle's dainty legs, as shown.

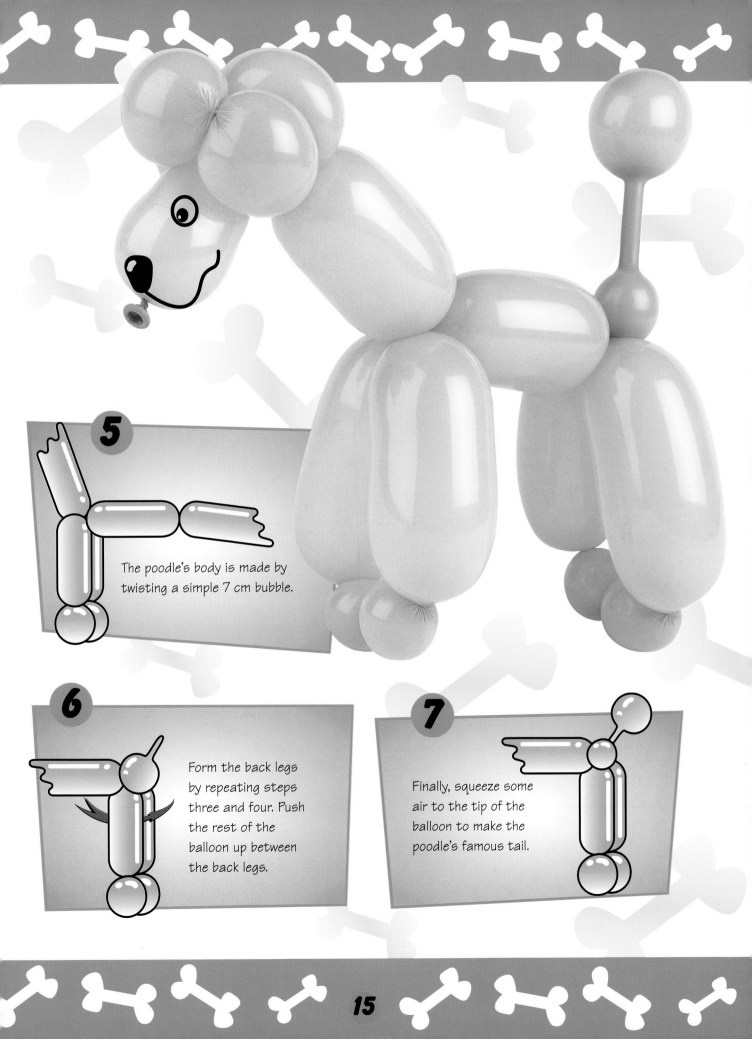

5

The poodle's body is made by twisting a simple 7 cm bubble.

6

Form the back legs by repeating steps three and four. Push the rest of the balloon up between the back legs.

7

Finally, squeeze some air to the tip of the balloon to make the poodle's famous tail.

Sword and Shield

Take up the challenge to make a fun sword and shield set. It's best to follow our colour guide first and then experiment with your favourite colours after!

YOU WILL NEED:
Sword
One long balloon
Shield
Four long balloons
Scissors

1

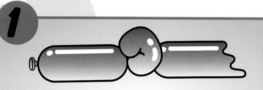

To make the sword, inflate the balloon and leave an 8 cm tip. Twist a 20 cm bubble, followed by a 4 cm bubble. Ear twist the small bubble.

2

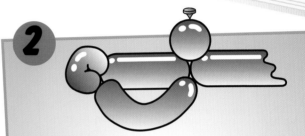

To make the handle and hand guard, curve the 20 cm bubble round. Lock twist it where it crosses the rest of the balloon, so that the knot now sits on a small bubble at the top. Make sure you leave enough room to grip the handle.

3

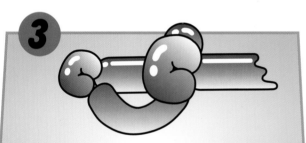

Ear twist two 10 cm bubbles to form the finger guards. Position them at right angles to the hand guard. Tuck in the knot. Squeeze the air along the blade to fill the sword.

Tip
You may find it helps to hold some part of these large models between your legs to free up your hands.

4

For the shield, inflate the long green balloon, leaving a 5 cm tip. Find the middle and ear twist a 4 cm bubble. Blow up a long red balloon, leave a 15 cm tip, then twist the centre of the green balloon onto the red one, a third of the way from the knotted end. You should now have a cross.

5

Add a 4 cm ear twist in the red balloon to lock the arms of the cross in position. Deflate and tie off the green balloon, ensuring that the two arms are the same length.

6

Take a long blue balloon, inflate it to leave a 5 cm tip, then tie its knot to the top of the cross. Bring the blue balloon across to one end of the cross bar and ear twist a 3 cm bubble where they meet. Lock twist this bubble to the tip of the cross bar.

7

Curve the rest of the balloon down to the bottom of the cross and lock twist it into position, making a 2 cm bubble in the red balloon. Repeat with the last blue balloon to complete the shield. Deflate, tie off and cut away any surplus balloon.

Flower Power

Surprise someone you know with a big bunch of tulips picked especially for them. These flowers will certainly brighten their day!

1

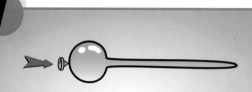

Inflate a 6 cm bubble and tie a knot. Push the knot back inside and press it right to the end of the bubble.

2

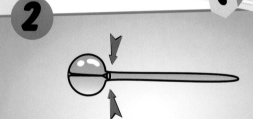

Grab the knot inside the deflated part of the bubble and double twist it to secure the knot.

3

Now push the knot back into the bubble to secure the twist and complete the flower head. This is the apple twist. The rest of the deflated balloon becomes the stem.

Tip
Tie a bouquet by inflating a long balloon to 6 cm. First, make sure the ends of the stalks line up neatly. Lock twist the bubble around the stalks, then tie off as usual.

Delightful Daisy

You can put on a flower show with these wonderful nodding daisies. Planting each one in its own balloon pot will help to keep them upright.

YOU WILL NEED:

Two long balloons

Scissors

1

To create the centre of the daisy, make a tulip head as before and leave a 4 cm stalk. Now inflate the pink balloon and leave a 15 cm tip. Tie the yellow bubble to the knot of the pink balloon.

2

Twist an 8 cm bubble in the pink balloon and ear twist it to form a petal. Repeat this step to make three more petals.

3

Position the petals around the yellow bubble. Leave a 3 cm bubble behind the flower and squeeze air to the base of the stem to finish your flower.

Tip
Make a flower pot with a 10 cm bubble. Wrap the bubble around the base of the daisy, then twist, tie off and tidy the ends.

Terrible Tiger

Once you have got to grips with this fantastic tiger, you can twist lots of different cats: black panthers, leopards, cheetahs, even your friendly tabby.

1

To make the head, inflate one balloon to leave a 10 cm tip, then tie off. Twist a 3 cm bubble and a 4 cm bubble, then lock twist them together. Tuck the knot between the two bubbles.

2

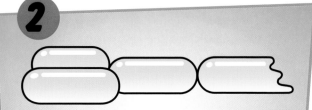

Now twist a 4 cm bubble. This will become the back of the tiger's head.

3

Next, twist a 5 cm bubble, a 2 cm bubble, a 5 cm bubble, a 2 cm bubble and a 5 cm bubble. Lock twist the first and last bubbles in this series together.

4

Push the two bubbles at the knotted end through the ring you have just made. Give the tiger ears by ear twisting the two small bubbles as shown. The head is now finished.

5

To make the neck and front legs, twist a 4 cm bubble, followed by two 8 cm bubbles. Lock twist these last two bubbles together.

6

Now twist an 8 cm bubble for the body, then two more 8 cm bubbles. Lock twist the last two together to form the rear legs.

7

Push the rest of the balloon up between the back legs to make the tiger's long tail. Use a felt pen to draw scary stripes on the tiger's face and body. Grrr!

Tip
To make the tiger lie down, gently pull the rear legs towards the front, then push the tail end of the body down between the back legs.

Penguin Parade

To make a penguin like ours, choose three long balloons in black, white and orange. Don't throw away any leftovers, as they come in handy later!

YOU WILL NEED:

Three long balloons

Scissors

Felt pen

1

Inflate the orange balloon to leave a 5 cm tip. Squeeze the air right to the end and twist a 5 cm bubble at the tip. Deflate, tie off, and cut a 1 cm stalk, saving the rest for later.

2

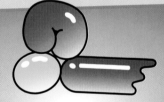

Inflate the black balloon and leave a 15 cm tip. Tie the orange bubble to the knot of the black balloon. Now twist a 10 cm bubble in the black balloon and ear twist it.

3

Twist two 12 cm wing bubbles and lock twist them together. Add another 10 cm bubble and push it between the 12 cm bubbles. Twist a 4 cm bubble, then deflate the rest of the balloon, tie off, and remove any surplus.

Tip
Use a felt pen to add eyes to your pet penguin, and draw a smile along his orange beak.

4

Inflate the white balloon and leave a 15 cm tip. Now twist two 4 cm bubbles and lock twist them together, then secure the knot. Push these bubbles through the penguin's head loop.

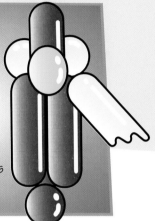

5

Twist a white 12 cm bubble for the chest and lock twist it to the small bubble at the bottom of the body. Twist a 3 cm bubble, deflate, then tie off and tidy the end. Tuck the small white bubble inside the body to secure the twists.

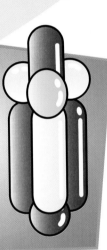

6

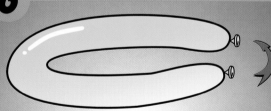

Make the feet from the spare orange balloon. Tie a knot to seal the cut end, then inflate a 30 cm bubble. Deflate and tie off. Trim the ends, leaving enough stalk to tie both ends together to make a loop.

7

Twist the loop into a figure of eight and lock twist the centre knot around the small bubble at the base of the body.

Prize Pony

Take first prize at the Pony Club with this pretty pony. We have used yellow and blue balloons, but you can choose your favourite colours.

YOU WILL NEED:

Two long balloons

Felt pen

Scissors

1 Inflate one balloon, leaving a 15 cm tip. Make the head with a 6 cm bubble. Then, twist a 3 cm bubble and ear twist it. Repeat with another 3 cm bubble.

2 Twist a 6 cm bubble for the neck. Now twist two 10 cm bubbles and lock twist them together for the front legs. Add a 10 cm bubble to make the body.

3

To form the rear legs, twist two more 10 cm bubbles and lock twist them together.

4

Push the rest of the balloon down between the back legs. Ear twist a 2 cm bubble to hold the tail in position.

5

To make the pony's mane, inflate the second balloon to 20 cm. Form a chain of eight bubbles by twisting a series of 2 cm bubbles. Hold the chain firmly!

6

Tie a knot after the last bubble, then tie the two knots of the bubble chain to make a ring. Deflate the rest of the balloon, tie off and save the scrap piece for the next step.

7

Put the ring on the pony's forehead, so it hangs in front of his chest. Push back the bubbles at the top of the head, and at the base of the neck, to form a double row of bubbles along the neck. Take the balloon scrap and tie it around the pony's nose and neck to keep the mane in position.

Tip
To stop the bubbles from coming undone, make sure that you put at least a double twist in between each one.

Ladybird Trail

To make this trail of ladybirds you will be twisting a lot of small bubbles. If your balloon is hard to twist, letting a little air out of it will help.

YOU WILL NEED:

One long balloon

Felt pen

1

Inflate your balloon to make a 24 cm bubble and tie off. Twist a 4 cm bubble for the head and wrap the knot around the twist. Secure the bubble by tucking the knot into the twist.

2

Now twist a row of six 2 cm bubbles. Don't let go before you lock twist the first and last small bubbles together to make a loop!

Tip
Add the dark markings to each ladybird with a black felt pen.

3

Next, twist a 5 cm bubble for the body. Push this large bubble through the loop, so that the legs sit on either side. Repeat the complete set of twists, with smaller bubbles, to make two more little ladybirds.

Speedy Snail

Not all snails are slow; just look at Speedy here. You'll find this out when you make him in four quick steps.

YOU WILL NEED:

One long balloon

12 cm scrap balloon

Felt pen

1

Inflate the green balloon to leave a 3 cm tip. Twist a 4 cm bubble for the head, followed by two 2 cm bubbles, each of which is ear twisted to form ear shapes.

2

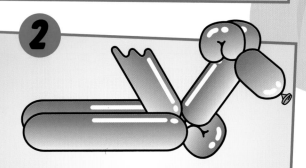

Now twist a 10 cm bubble for the neck, followed by a 3 cm ear twisted bubble. Next, twist two 15 cm bubbles and lock twist them at the base of the neck.

3

Starting at the tip end, roll the remaining bubble into a tight coil and push it partway between the two lock twisted bubbles to form the snail's shell.

4

Tie a knot in one end of the scrap balloon. Blow air into it to make a tube, then tie off. Wrap the tube behind the ears and pull the ends up between the ear twists to make feelers.

Party Time!

Who can make the craziest party hat? Have a go at this antennae hat, and then use your imagination to invent something new!

YOU WILL NEED:

Three long balloons
One large round balloon
Felt pen

1

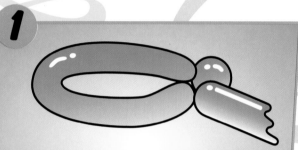

Inflate a long balloon and leave a 4 cm tip. Wrap the balloon around your head to get a loop the size of your head. Lift the loop and lock twist it, with a 3 cm bubble overlapping at the knot end.

2

Twist a 10 cm bubble. This will be the support for the main feature of the hat. Next, twist a 12 cm bubble and bend it over to ear twist it.

3

You should now be getting close to the end of the balloon. Twist two final 4 cm bubbles and ear twist each one. Adjust them to hold the 12 cm bubble up as shown.

Tip
Why not make hats for your friends and family for other special occasions? If you get the head loop right, the rest will follow!

4

Inflate the round balloon to the size of a tennis ball. Twist the balloon in half and push it into the loop at the top of the hat.

5

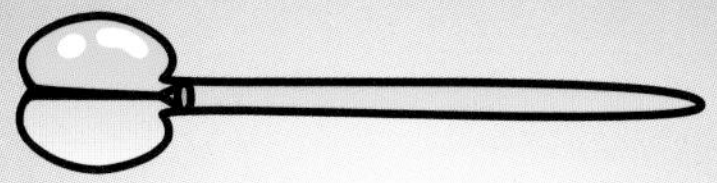

Now inflate a 7 cm bubble in a yellow balloon. Apple twist this bubble, making sure that the knot is secure. Push the knot back into the bubble to make a distinct apple shape.

6

To create one wacky antenna, twist the stalk of the yellow balloon around one of the small ear twists.

7

Repeat steps five and six to make the other antenna. Secure it to the other ear twist in the same way. Now you can draw on some eyes with a felt pen to complete your crazy party hat!

Scary Spider

Sadly, this extremely rare four-legged spider is now seldom seen – unless, of course, you make one for yourself...

YOU WILL NEED:

Two thin balloons
One large round balloon
Scissors

1

To make the legs, inflate a long balloon and leave a 10 cm tip. Twist a 4 cm bubble, wrap the knot around the twist, then hide the knot. Ear twist a 2 cm bubble to secure the twists. This is one foot.

2

Twist a 12 cm bubble, then add another ear twisted 2 cm bubble. Next, twist an 8 cm bubble, and a 2 cm ear twisted bubble.

3

Add an 8 cm bubble, followed by a 2 cm bubble. Ear twist this bubble, then twist a 12 cm bubble, followed by a further 2 cm ear twisted bubble for the heel.

4

Finish the legs by ear twisting a 4 cm bubble. Deflate, tie off and secure as usual.

Tip
Balloons are quite robust, so don't be afraid to twist and squash them to make these models.

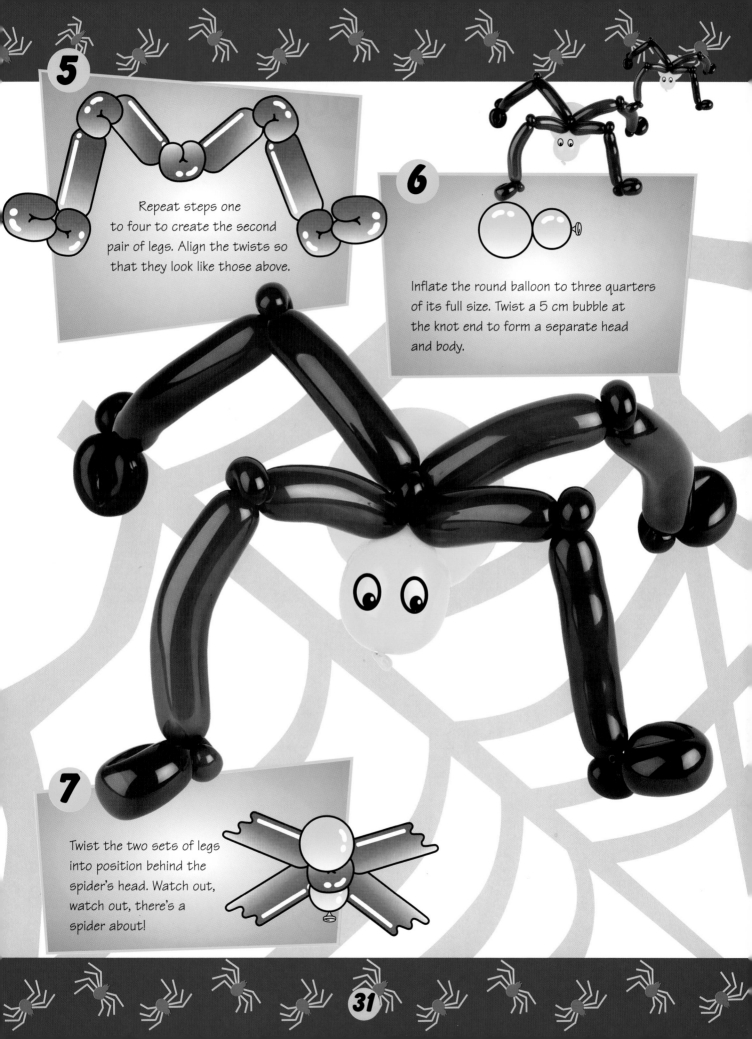

5

Repeat steps one to four to create the second pair of legs. Align the twists so that they look like those above.

6

Inflate the round balloon to three quarters of its full size. Twist a 5 cm bubble at the knot end to form a separate head and body.

7

Twist the two sets of legs into position behind the spider's head. Watch out, watch out, there's a spider about!

Daring Dog

Roll up! Roll up! Please make yourself comfortable during the amazing antics of the only performing motorcycle stunt dog in the world!

YOU WILL NEED:

One long balloon

Felt pen

1

Inflate the balloon, leave a 15 cm tip and tie off. Twist a 5 cm bubble, followed by three 3 cm bubbles. Lock twist the first and last 3 cm bubbles together to form a ring. Push the first bubble partway through the ring to form the nose.

2

Next, twist five 2 cm bubbles. Lock twist the second and last together to make the neck and arms. Create the body with a 6 cm bubble.

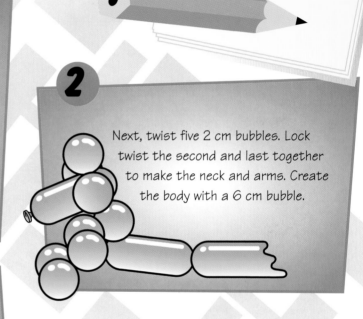

3

Make a 12 cm bubble and ear twist it, followed by a 6 cm ear twisted bubble. Push this last bubble halfway into the loop of the 12 cm ear twist to form a wheel.

4

Continue making the motorcycle by twisting a 7 cm bubble, then a 6 cm bubble. Ear twist the last bubble.

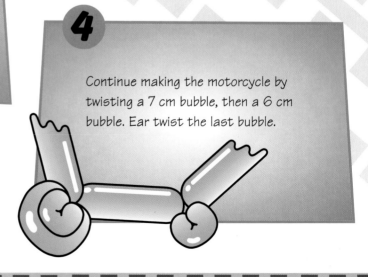

Tip
Check that the positions of your twists and bubbles match those in the diagrams.

5

Squeeze the air to fill the balloon, then twist a final 12 cm bubble, leaving a small 2 cm bubble at the tip of the balloon.

6

Ear twist the 12 cm bubble, then make the second wheel by pushing the ear twisted 6 cm bubble from step four into this loop.

7

Secure the model by pushing the tip bubble up between the handlebars, so that it looks like a headlamp. Add some details with a felt pen!

Space Bug

YOU WILL NEED:

Four long balloons
10 cm scrap balloon
Felt pen
Scissors

An alien has just landed and this is what he looks like. Why is he here? What on earth does he want? Most importantly of all: is he friendly?

1

Take a yellow balloon and inflate it, leaving a 5 cm tip. Twist two 8 cm bubbles, lock twist them together and hide the knot. Next, ear twist a 3 cm bubble.

2

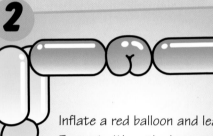

Inflate a red balloon and leave a 5 cm tip. Wrap the knot around the top twist in the yellow balloon and tuck in the knot. Next, twist an 8 cm bubble for the nose, then ear twist a 3 cm bubble.

3

Twist the two ear twists together so the small yellow bubble sits below the red nose, and the red ear twist is at the back of the head.

4

Lock twist the balloons together to form a 7 cm neck bubble. To finish the body, squeeze and curve the balloons around each other several times as shown. Lock twist them together at the end to secure.

5

Inflate a long balloon and leave a 6 cm tip. Twist an 8 cm bubble, ear twist it and hide the knot. Ear twist a 3 cm bubble for the heel of the foot. Twist a 10 cm bubble, then ear twist a 3 cm bubble for the knee. Add a 6 cm bubble, then a central 3 cm ear twisted bubble.

6

Continue twisting the balloon in reverse order to finish the pair of legs; the next bubble will be a 6 cm bubble, and so on. Tie off, deflate and remove any scrap balloon. Make another pair of legs, then lock twist one pair to the base of the neck and the other towards the end of the body.

7

To add eyes, inflate a white balloon to 12 cm and tie off. Twist two 4 cm bubbles, then lock twist them together. Deflate, tie off and save any leftover balloon. Insert the eyes between the top twist in the head bubble.

8

Tie a knot in the end of the scrap balloon. Blow in a little air to form a tube and tie off. Tie a knot in the middle and thread the feeler behind the eyes.

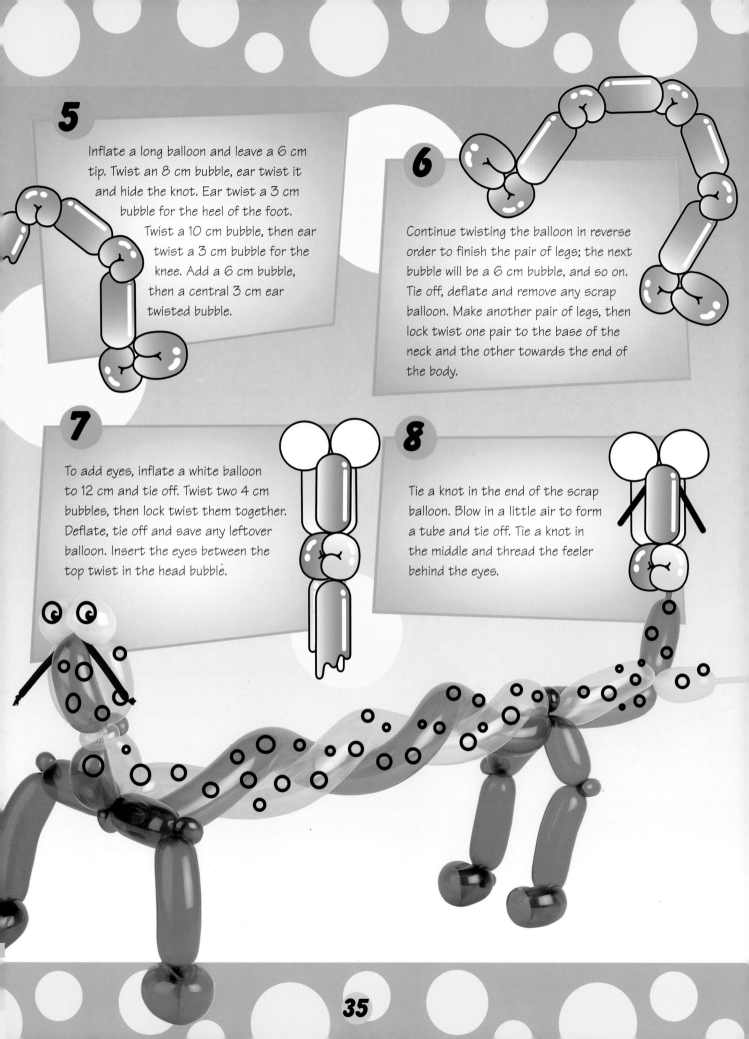

Batmania

Transform your room into a real bat cave by hanging lots of flying bats from the ceiling – what a great idea for a Hallowe'en theme party!

YOU WILL NEED:

One long balloon
Scissors
White paper
Sticky tape
Felt tip

1

Inflate the balloon to 70 cm. Create the bat's head by pushing the knot 3 cm back inside the balloon, pinch the knot through the balloon and twist the bubble to make an apple twist.

2

Next, twist two 2 cm bubbles and ear twist them to form the eyes. The head is now complete.

3

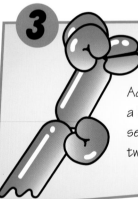

Add a neck by twisting a 3 cm bubble, then secure this by ear twisting a 2 cm bubble.

4

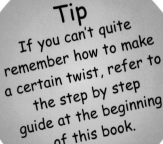

To make the wings, twist a bubble about 10 cm from the end of the inflated section. Ear twist the long bubble to the base of the bat's neck.

Tip
If you can't quite remember how to make a certain twist, refer to the step by step guide at the beginning of this book.

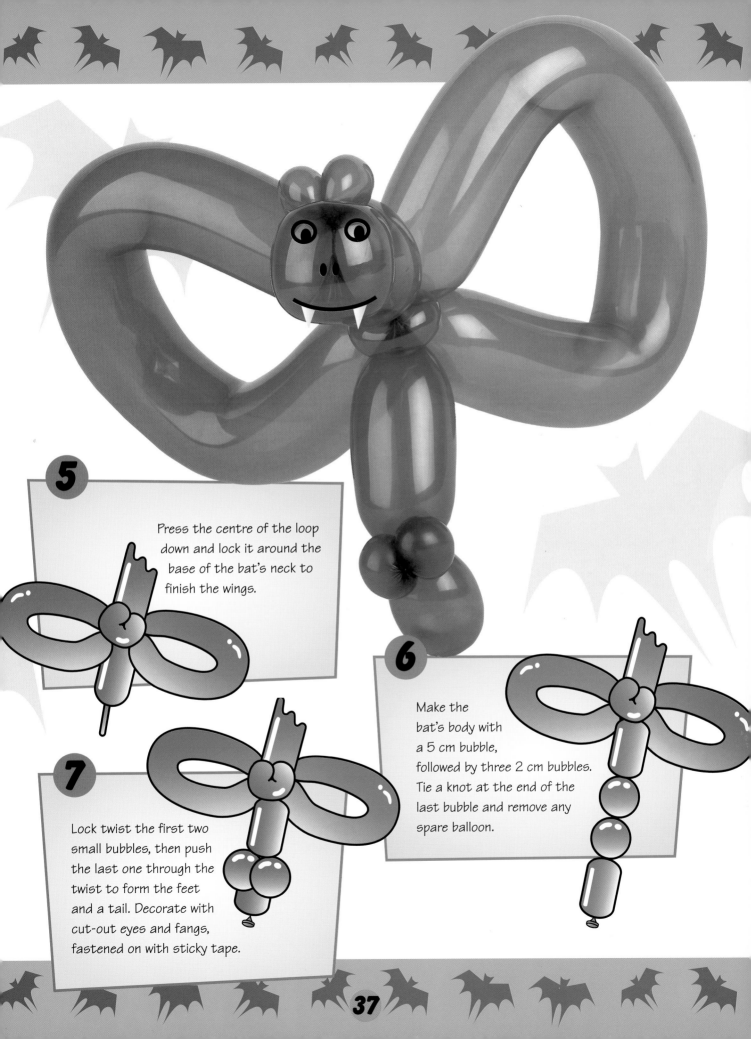

5

Press the centre of the loop down and lock it around the base of the bat's neck to finish the wings.

6

Make the bat's body with a 5 cm bubble, followed by three 2 cm bubbles. Tie a knot at the end of the last bubble and remove any spare balloon.

7

Lock twist the first two small bubbles, then push the last one through the twist to form the feet and a tail. Decorate with cut-out eyes and fangs, fastened on with sticky tape.

Sea Horse

This sleek sea horse looks very impressive, but is easier to make than it looks. Choose transparent bubbles for an underwater effect!

YOU WILL NEED:

One long balloon
One thin balloon
8 cm scrap balloon
Felt pen
Scissors

1

Inflate the long balloon, leaving a 12 cm tip. Twist a 6 cm bubble, followed by two 2 cm bubbles. Ear twist the two small bubbles.

2

Twist a 5 cm bubble, then ear twist a 2 cm bubble. To make the body, twist a 20 cm bubble and, holding it at each end, move your hands to and fro along the bubble to produce a good curve.

3

Ear twist a 3 cm bubble, then twist a 3 cm bubble. Now add a 2 cm ear twisted bubble and then twist a 3 cm bubble.

4

Finish the main body with a 2 cm ear twisted bubble, and then a 2 cm bubble. Deflate the rest of the balloon, tie a knot and trim off the leftover balloon.

5

Inflate the thin balloon to leave a 10 cm tip. Tie the knot round the sea horse's ears. Twist four 2 cm bubbles. Lock twist the last one to the small bubble at the base of the sea horse's neck.

6

Continue making 2 cm bubbles down the sea horse's body, then lock twist the last one in the chain to the end of the body. Deflate, tie off and trim away any spare balloon.

7

Take the scrap piece of balloon and tie it round the belly of the sea horse to keep the bubbles close to the body. Add a face and some scales with a felt pen.

Tip
When twisting a long chain of bubbles, you only need to keep the first and last in your hand. The other bubbles will be locked by those on either side.

Rock Lobster

This fearsome fellow lives amongst the rocks on the sea bed and has a reputation for being able to look after himself, so mind those pincer arms!

YOU WILL NEED:

Three long red balloons
Three long black balloons
12 cm scrap balloon
Scissors
Felt pen

1

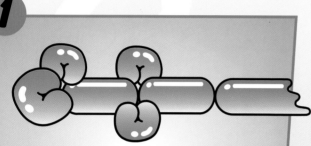

Inflate one long red balloon and leave a 15 cm tip. Twist a 15 cm bubble, wrap the knot round the twist and hide it. Next, ear twist a 3 cm bubble, add a 7 cm bubble, two ear twisted 3 cm bubbles, then a 6 cm bubble.

2

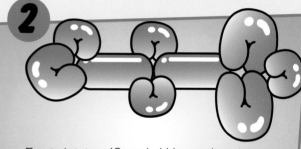

Ear twist two 12 cm bubbles and position them opposite each other. Finish with a 3 cm bubble, ear twist it, then secure. Deflate, tie off, secure and remove any surplus balloon.

3

Inflate another long red balloon as before. Twist a 3 cm bubble, then a 5 cm bubble. Wrap the knot round the last twist. Tuck in the knot, then ear twist a 2 cm bubble.

4

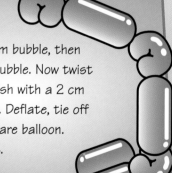

Next, twist an 8 cm bubble, then ear twist a 2 cm bubble. Now twist a 6 cm bubble. Finish with a 2 cm ear twisted bubble. Deflate, tie off and remove any spare balloon. Secure with a knot.

5

Repeat steps three and four to make the other arm. Lock twist the last small bubble of each arm behind the head.

6

Tie a knot at the tip of one dark balloon. Blow a little air into it to make a tube. Tie a knot in the middle, then twist to the body as shown. Repeat with the other two dark balloons.

7

The antennae are created by making a 12 cm tube from the scrap balloon and twisting it just behind the head, with the antennae pointing upwards.

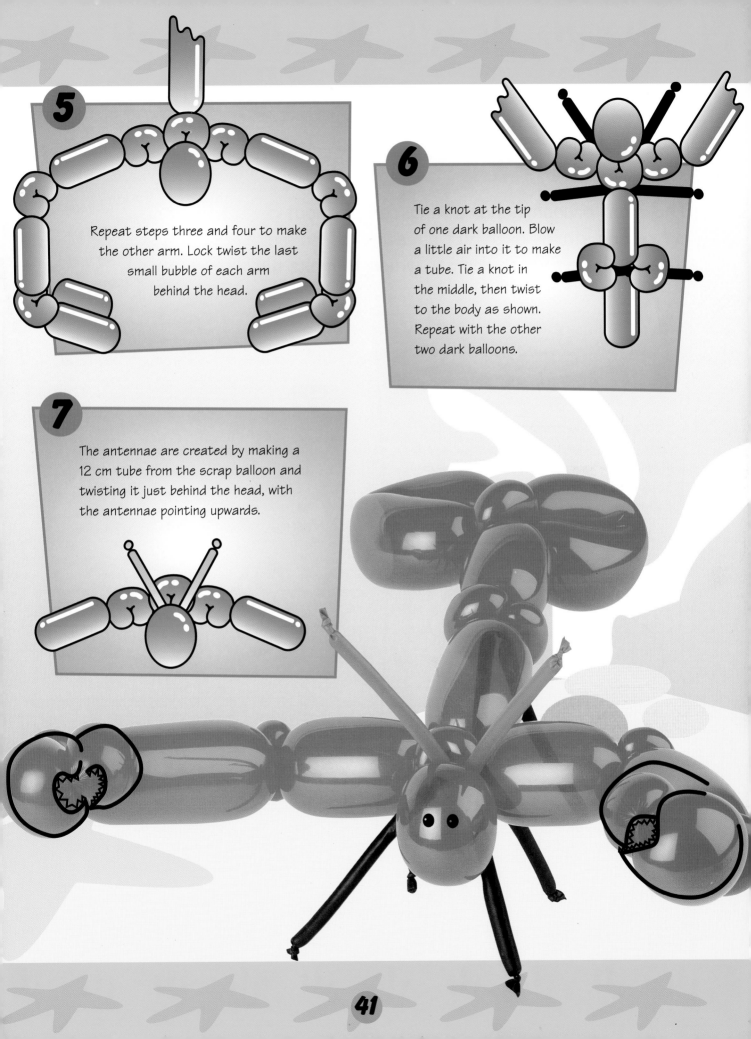

Dizzy Dragonfly

This giant dragonfly has a wingspan of about a metre and stands over half a metre tall, so make sure you have enough room in which to make him!

YOU WILL NEED:

Five long balloons
Three thin balloons
14 cm scrap balloon
Scissors

1

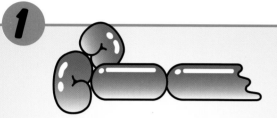

Begin the body by inflating a dark balloon to leave a 6 cm tip. Twist a 5 cm bubble and wrap the knot round the twist. Next, ear twist a 3 cm bubble and follow it with an 8 cm bubble.

2

To make a body section, ear twist two 3 cm bubbles, then twist a 4 cm bubble. Repeat this step to make another body section, then ear twist two more 3 cm bubbles. The last bubble forms the tail.

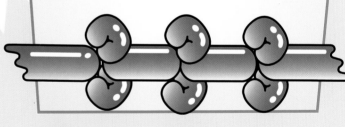

3

Next, inflate a pale or transparent balloon and leave a 2 cm tip. Fold the balloon in half and squeeze the bend to make a slender wing shape. Tie the tip of the balloon to its knot.

4

Inflate a second pale balloon to leave a 2 cm tip. Thread this balloon through the first wing. Tie its knot to its tip to link the two balloons. Shape this wing as the first, then lock twist the knots together.

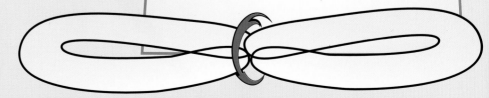

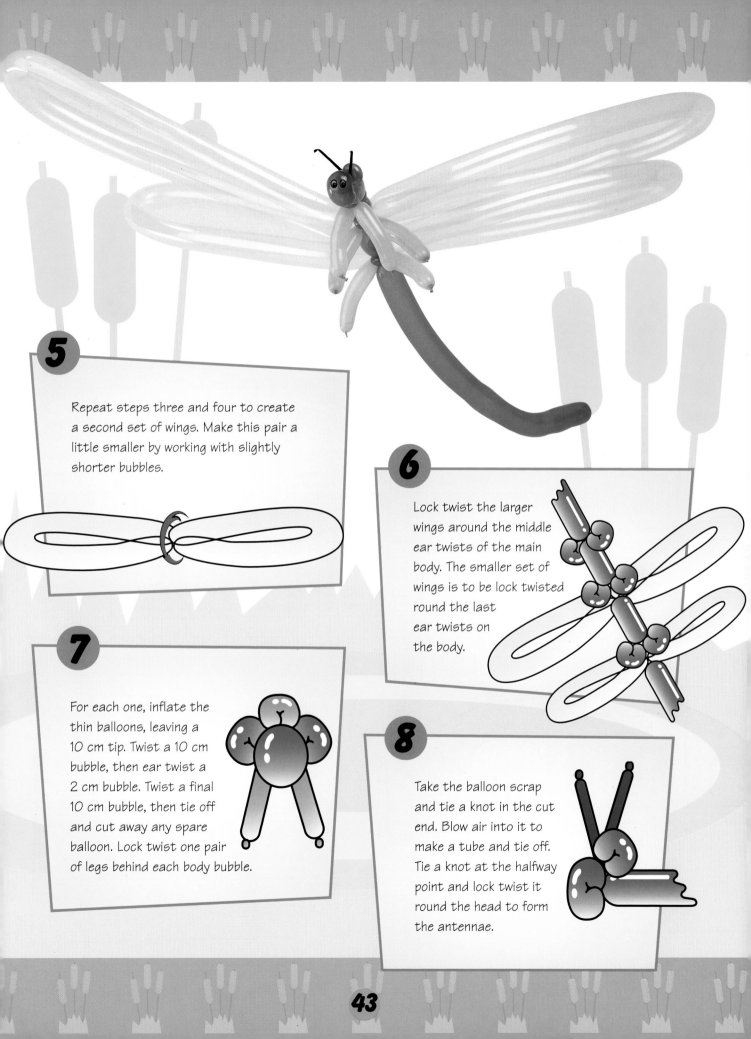

5

Repeat steps three and four to create a second set of wings. Make this pair a little smaller by working with slightly shorter bubbles.

6

Lock twist the larger wings around the middle ear twists of the main body. The smaller set of wings is to be lock twisted round the last ear twists on the body.

7

For each one, inflate the thin balloons, leaving a 10 cm tip. Twist a 10 cm bubble, then ear twist a 2 cm bubble. Twist a final 10 cm bubble, then tie off and cut away any spare balloon. Lock twist one pair of legs behind each body bubble.

8

Take the balloon scrap and tie a knot in the cut end. Blow air into it to make a tube and tie off. Tie a knot at the halfway point and lock twist it round the head to form the antennae.

Baby Elephant

YOU WILL NEED:

Two long balloons

Felt pen

Here's another interesting animal for your wildlife collection. If you team him up with the giraffe, you can imagine them in Africa...

1

To make the head, inflate one balloon, leaving only a 5 cm tip. Twist a 20 cm bubble and make a loop by lock twisting the knot at the end of the bubble.

2

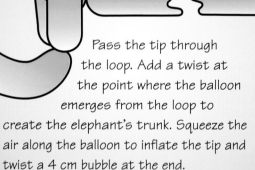

Pass the tip through the loop. Add a twist at the point where the balloon emerges from the loop to create the elephant's trunk. Squeeze the air along the balloon to inflate the tip and twist a 4 cm bubble at the end.

3

Make another large loop by lock twisting the 4 cm bubble to the back of the head.

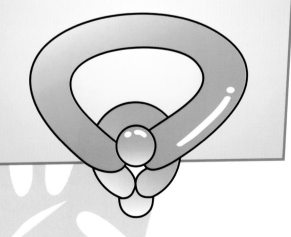

4

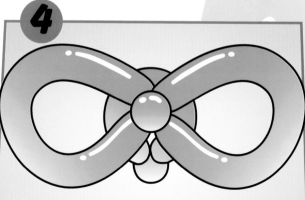

Press the middle of the loop down to form a figure of eight and lock twist it to the 4 cm bubble.

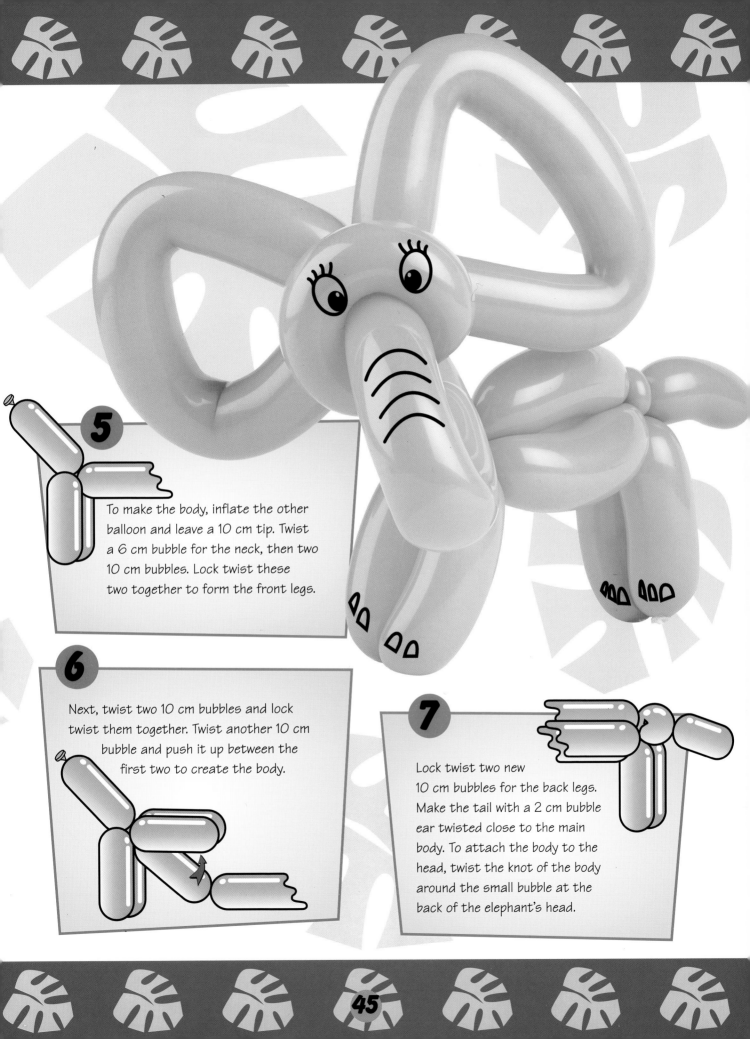

5

To make the body, inflate the other balloon and leave a 10 cm tip. Twist a 6 cm bubble for the neck, then two 10 cm bubbles. Lock twist these two together to form the front legs.

6

Next, twist two 10 cm bubbles and lock twist them together. Twist another 10 cm bubble and push it up between the first two to create the body.

7

Lock twist two new 10 cm bubbles for the back legs. Make the tail with a 2 cm bubble ear twisted close to the main body. To attach the body to the head, twist the knot of the body around the small bubble at the back of the elephant's head.

Jungle Fever

An orang-utan's favourite place is a leafy tree in the middle of the jungle. Now you can make him feel at home with you too!

1

Inflate a long balloon and leave a 10 cm tip. Twist a 4 cm bubble, a 2 cm bubble, then four 4 cm bubbles. Lock twist the second and last of the 4 cm bubbles together. Push the first bubble through the loop. Twist the knot round the base of the loop to form the back of the head as shown.

2

Twist a 3 cm bubble for the neck. Next, twist two 10 cm bubbles and lock twist them together. Make another 10 cm bubble and push it between the other two to form the orang-utan's body.

3

To make the legs, twist a 10 cm bubble, two 2 cm bubbles, then another 10 cm bubble. Lock twist the 10 cm bubbles together at the base of the body, then twist a 2 cm bubble at the back. Deflate, tie off and save any leftover scraps.

4

Now inflate the thin balloon, leaving a 15 cm tip. Twist four 2 cm bubbles, then lock twist the second and fourth. Push the first bubble though the middle to make a hand and hold the twists.

46

5

Now twist a 12 cm bubble, ear twist a 2 cm bubble, then add another 12 cm bubble. Repeat the twists in step four to make the other hand. Twist the middle bubble of the arms around the neck of the orang-utan.

6

Inflate the two tree balloons, leaving a 2 cm tip in each. Make a large loop in the green balloon by tying its knot to its tip, then twist it in the middle to form a double loop.

7

Wrap the knot of the trunk around the centre twist of the double loop. Add coconuts by ear twisting three 2 cm bubbles in the trunk.

8

Tie the knots in the orang-utan's hands together, then push the base of the trunk down through the arm and leg loops, so that he can climb the tree.

Tip

To make the base of the tree more stable, twist three 6 cm bubbles at the tip end. Ear twist each one and adjust them as necessary.

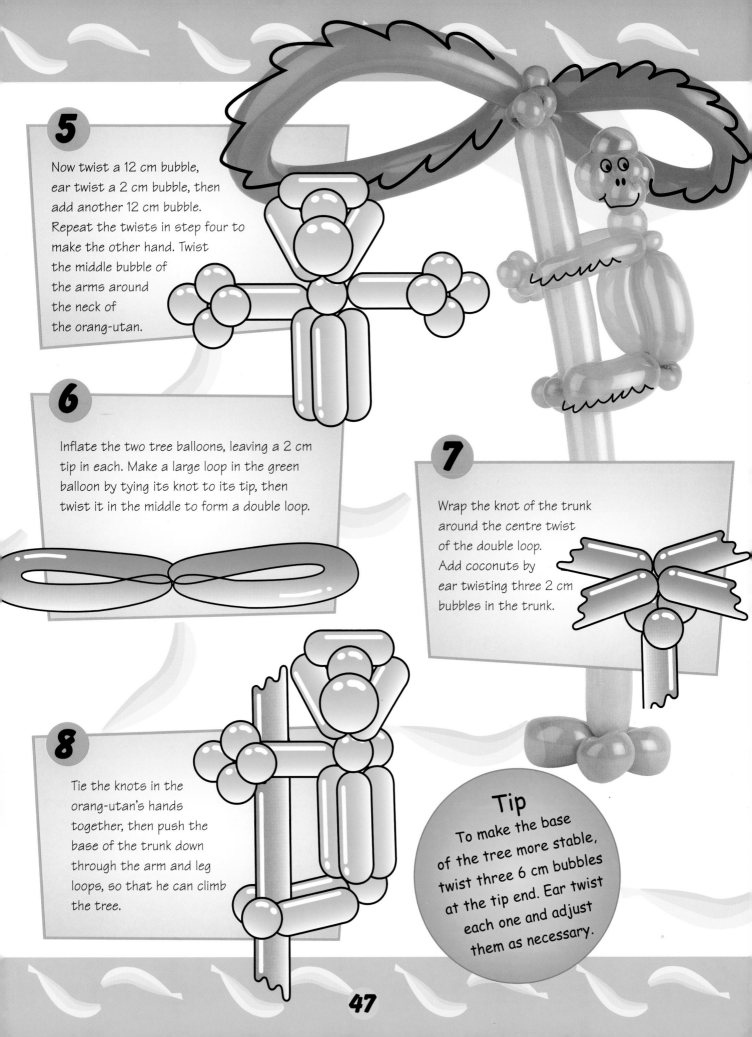

Exotic Octopus

How many arms does an octopus have? If you're not sure, you'll soon find out! Try using lots of different colours for a truly tropical look.

YOU WILL NEED:

Four long balloons
One large round balloon
Felt pen

1

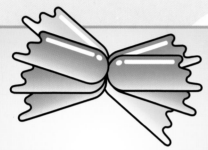

Inflate all of the long balloons and leave a 1 cm tip at the end of each one. Now line up the four balloons, find the midpoint and lock twist them all together to form the eight legs.

2

Inflate the round balloon to half of its size so it is a pear shape. Lock twist the knot of the round balloon to the middle twist of the sea creature's legs.

3

Bend the eight legs into curves. The more curves, the more alive your octopus will look. Finally add two big eyes with a felt pen.

Tip
A quick way to shape the curves is to wrap each balloon around your arm and squeeze the balloon with your other hand at the same time.